MARVEL

HOW TO DRAW

Awesome Characters

DK Penguin Random House

Editor Tracey Turner
Designers Peter Clayman and Andrew Bowden
Senior Production Editor Jen Murray
Senior Production Controller Laura Andrews
Managing Editor Rachel Lawrence
Publisher Paula Regan
Art Director Charlotte Coulais
Publishing Director Mark Searle

First American Edition, 2025
Published in the United States by DK Publishing, a division of Penguin Random House LLC
1745 Broadway, 20th Floor, New York, NY 10019
Page design copyright © 2025 Dorling Kindersley Limited

MARVEL

© 2025 MARVEL

25 26 27 28 29 10 9 8 7 6 5 4 3 2 1
001–349677–May/2025
All rights reserved.
Without limiting the rights under the copyright reserved above, no part of this publication may be reproduced, stored in or introduced into a retrieval system, or transmitted, in any form, or by any means (electronic, mechanical, photocopying, recording, or otherwise), without the prior written permission of the copyright owner.
Published in Great Britain by Dorling Kindersley Limited
No part of this publication may be used or reproduced in any manner for the purpose of training artificial intelligence technologies or systems. In accordance with Article 4(3) of the DSM Directive 2019/790, DK expressly reserves this work from the text and data mining exception.

A catalog record for this book is available from the Library of Congress.
ISBN 978-0-5939-6928-1

DK books are available at special discounts when purchased in bulk for sales promotions, premiums, fund-raising, or educational use. For details, contact: DK Publishing Special Markets, 1745 Broadway, 20th Floor, New York, NY 10019
SpecialSales@dk.com

Printed and bound in China
www.dk.com
www.marvel.com

MIX Paper | Supporting responsible forestry
FSC™ C018179

This book was made with Forest Stewardship Council™ certified paper – one small step in DK's commitment to a sustainable future.
Learn more at www.dk.com/uk/information/sustainability

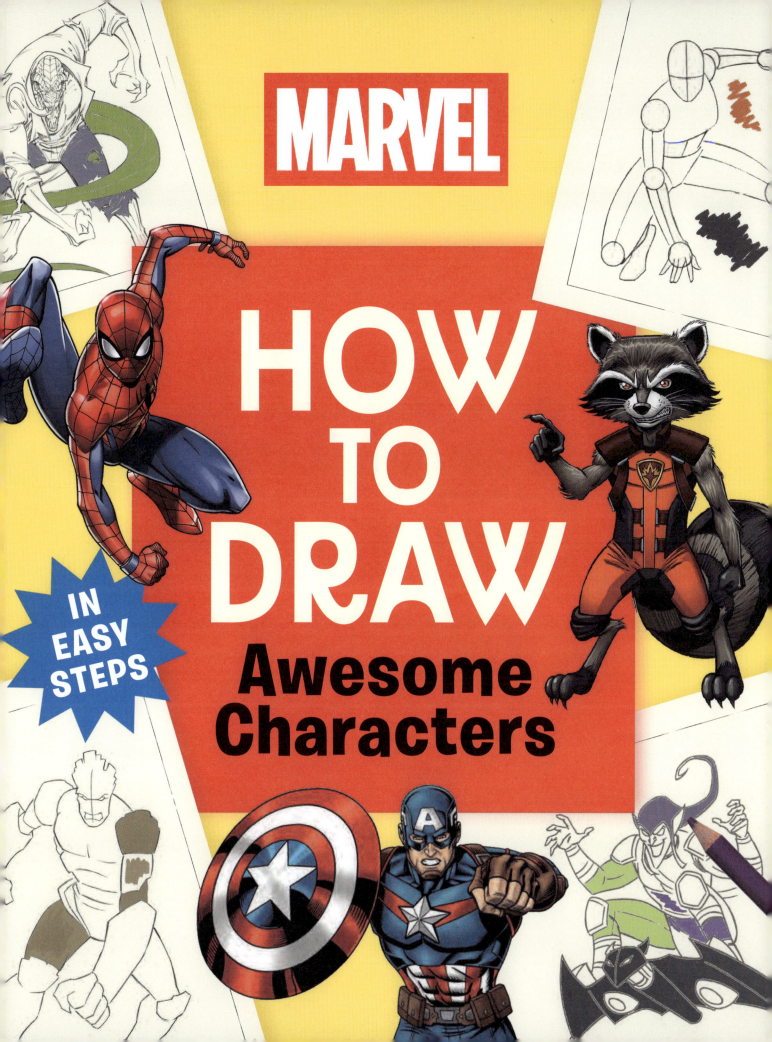

Contents

Tools and Materials **6**

Tracing Basics **7**

Grid Drawing Method **8**

Step-by-step Drawing Method **9**

Spider-Man **10**

Venom **20**

Lizard **30**

Green Goblin **38**

Rhino **44**

Doctor Octopus **50**

Iron Man **58**

Captain America	66
Black Widow	74
Hulk	82
Thor	90
Ant-Man	96
Black Panther	102
Captain Marvel	108
Star-Lord	114
Gamora	124
Rocket	130
Groot	136
Young Groot	142

Tools and Materials

You need to gather only a few simple art supplies before you begin. Start with a drawing pencil and an eraser. Make sure you also have a pencil sharpener and a ruler. To add color to your drawings, use markers, colored pencils, crayons, watercolors, or acrylic paint. The choice is yours!

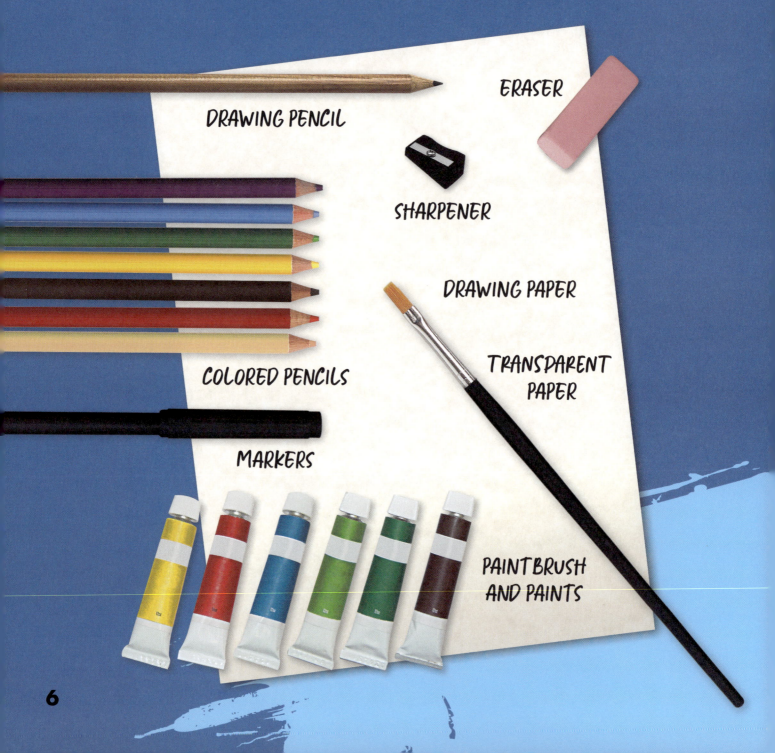

Tracing Basics

**Use blank transparent paper to trace the characters.
Then use color to bring them to life.**

1

← **transparent paper**

Make sure the transparent paper is placed over the character you want to draw. You should be able to see through the transparent paper.

2

With your pencil, draw everything you can see over the character you're tracing.

3

Pay close attention to all the little details. When you're done, transfer the traced image onto a blank sheet of paper by turning over the transparent paper and rubbing over the lines.

7

Grid Drawing Method

Divide a sheet of paper into squares, by drawing five evenly spaced lines going across the page (dividing it into six rows), and three evenly spaced lines going down the page (dividing it into four columns). Then focus on copying the lines and shapes in each square. The lines of the grid will help you draw your lines and shapes in the correct places.

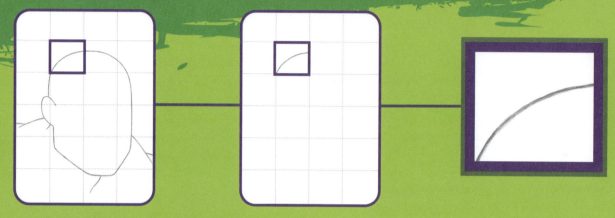

Copy everything you see in each square into the corresponding square on your blank practice grid. Make sure you are copying the shapes and lines into the correct spot!

After you've completed all the lines in step one, move on to the next step and keep going. Add color, and you're done!

Step-by-step Drawing Method

When using the step-by-step drawing method, begin by drawing very basic shapes, such as lines and circles. Then draw new lines as shown in each step.

1

First draw the basic shapes, using light lines that will be easy to erase.

2
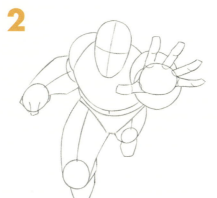

Pay attention to the new lines added in each step.

3

Erase guidelines and add more detail.

4

In each new step, add more defining lines.

5

Take your time adding detail and copying what you see.

6

Add color to your drawing with colored pencils, markers, paints, or crayons!

SPIDER-MAN

Bitten by a radioactive spider, high school student Peter Parker gains the speed, strength, and powers of a spider. Adopting the name **SPIDER-MAN**, Peter hopes to start a wrestling career using his new abilities. But he learns that with great power comes great responsibility, and Spidey vows to use his powers to help people instead.

SUPER-POWERS

* Can cling to most surfaces
* Has superhuman strength and agility
* Shoots long strands of adhesive fibers from his web-shooters
* Can travel quickly using acrobatic leaps and web-slinging
* Spider-sense provides an early warning detection system to evade injury

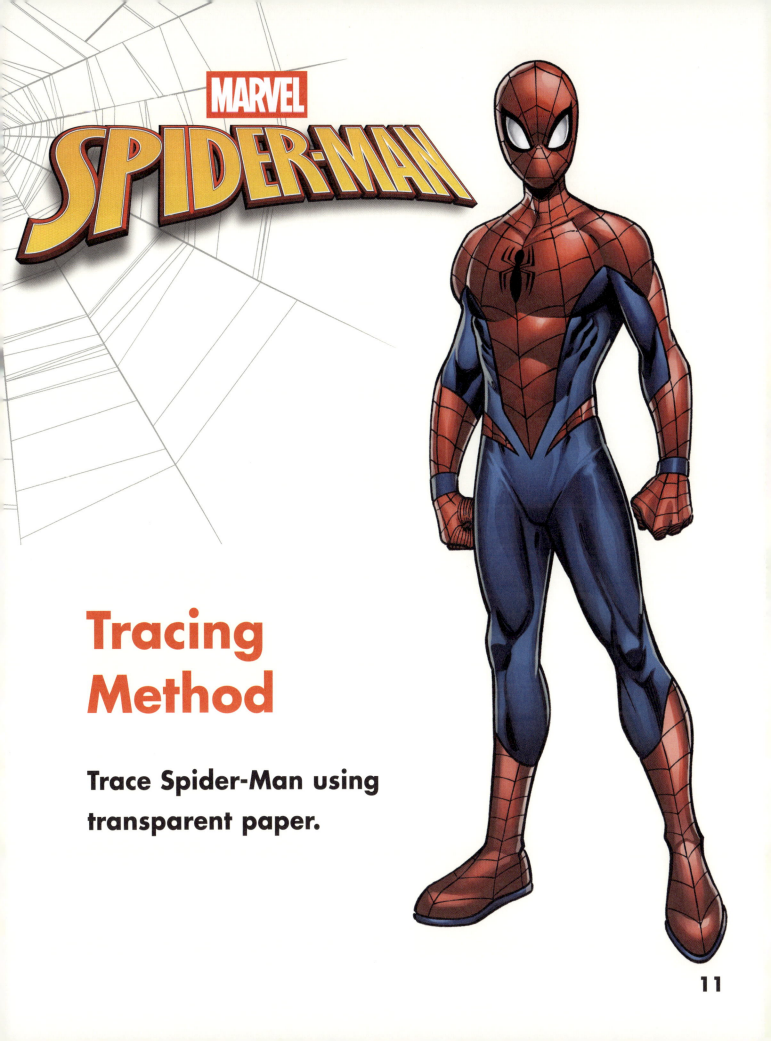

Tracing Method

Trace Spider-Man using transparent paper.

Grid Method

Copy the lines shown in each step. When you're done with all the steps, you'll have a complete drawing of Spider-Man. Color in your drawing with markers, colored pencils, crayons, or paints.

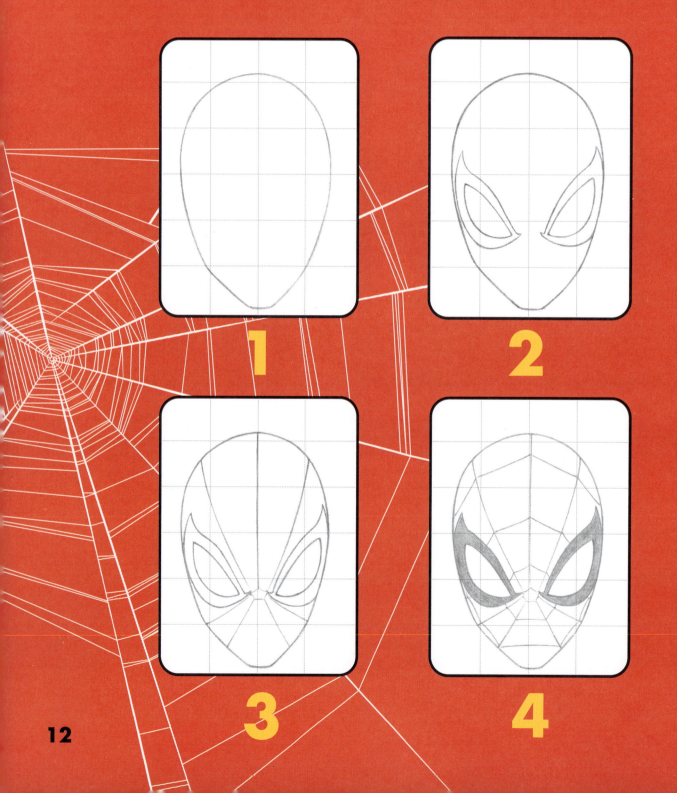

Step-by-step Method

Follow along, first drawing basic shapes with light pencil lines.

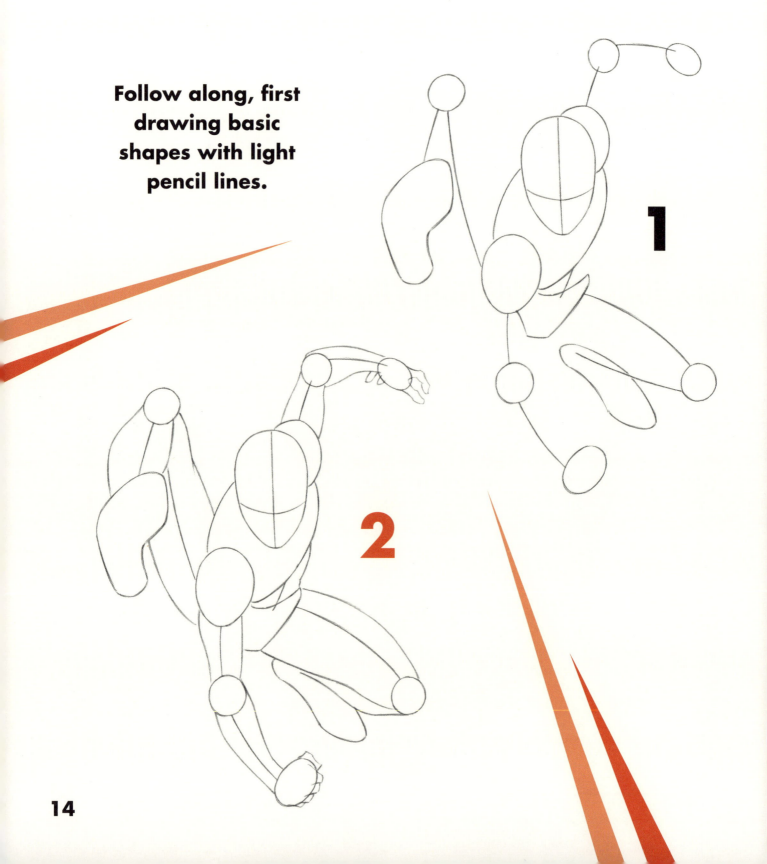

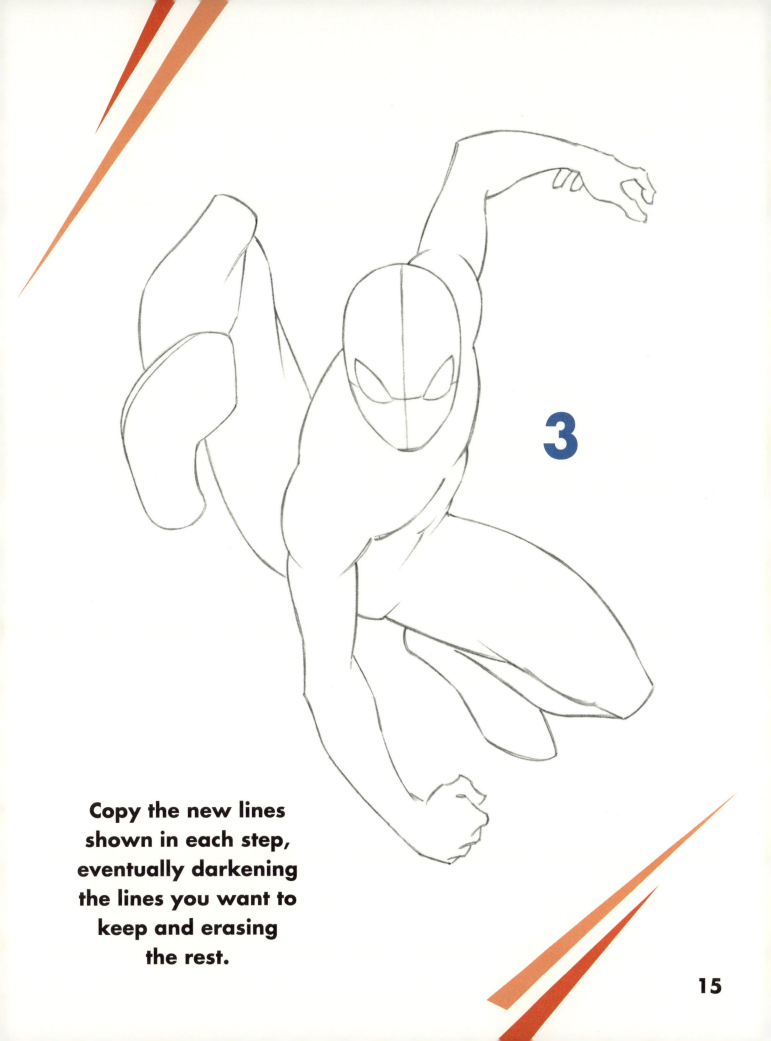

3

Copy the new lines shown in each step, eventually darkening the lines you want to keep and erasing the rest.

15

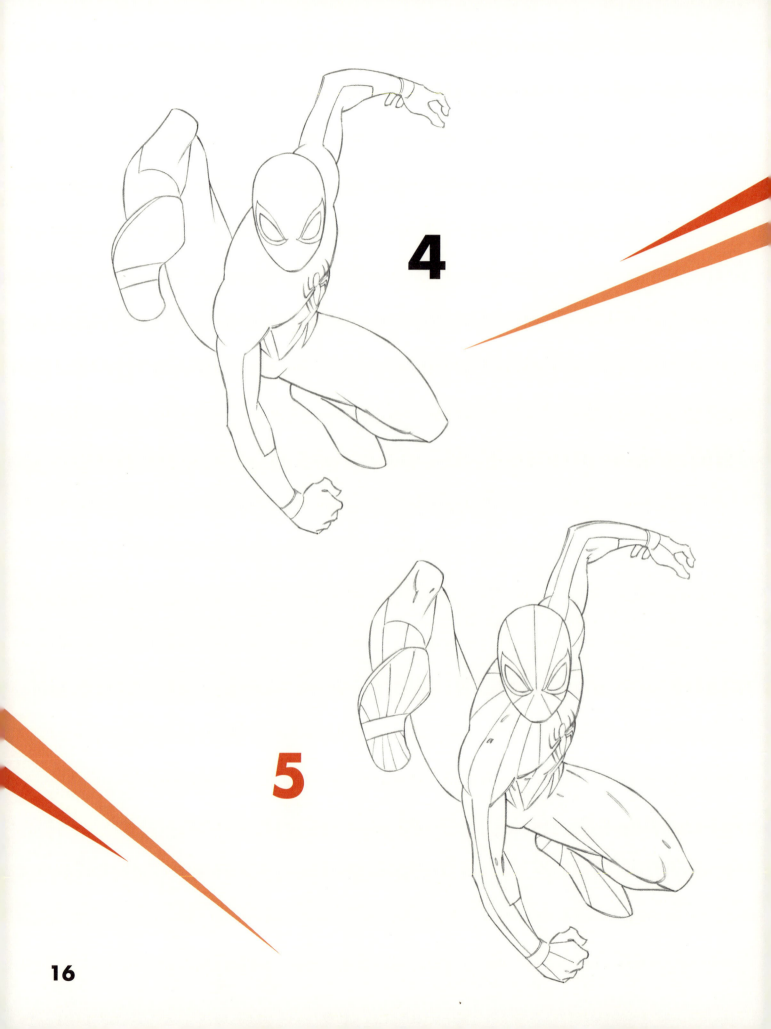

7

8

Add color to your drawing with colored pencils, markers, paints, or crayons.

VENOM

Eddie Brock, former *Daily Globe* journalist, blames Spider-Man for his troubled personal life. Eddie falls victim to a parasitic alien suit, which brings out the worst in its wearer, and is transformed into **VENOM**. Because the symbiote suit had previously attached itself to Spider-Man, Venom's abilities mimic those of Spider-Man.

SUPER-POWERS

* Augmented physical strength
* Can project organic webbing
* Extrasensory ability similar to Spider-Man's spider-sense
* Suit can absorb bullets and provide some camouflage

Tracing Method

Trace Venom using transparent paper.

Grid Method

Copy the lines shown in each step. When you're done with all the steps, you'll have a complete drawing of Venom. Color in your drawing with markers, colored pencils, crayons, or paints.

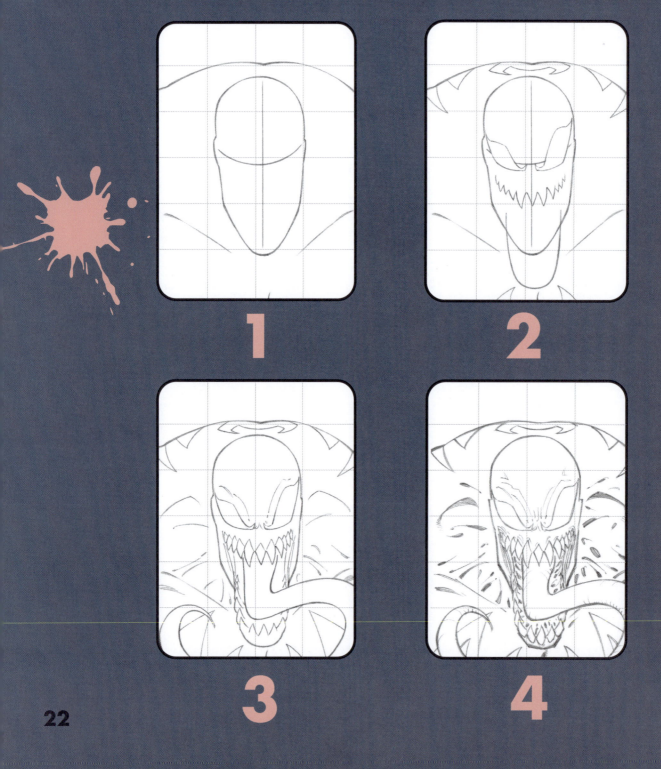

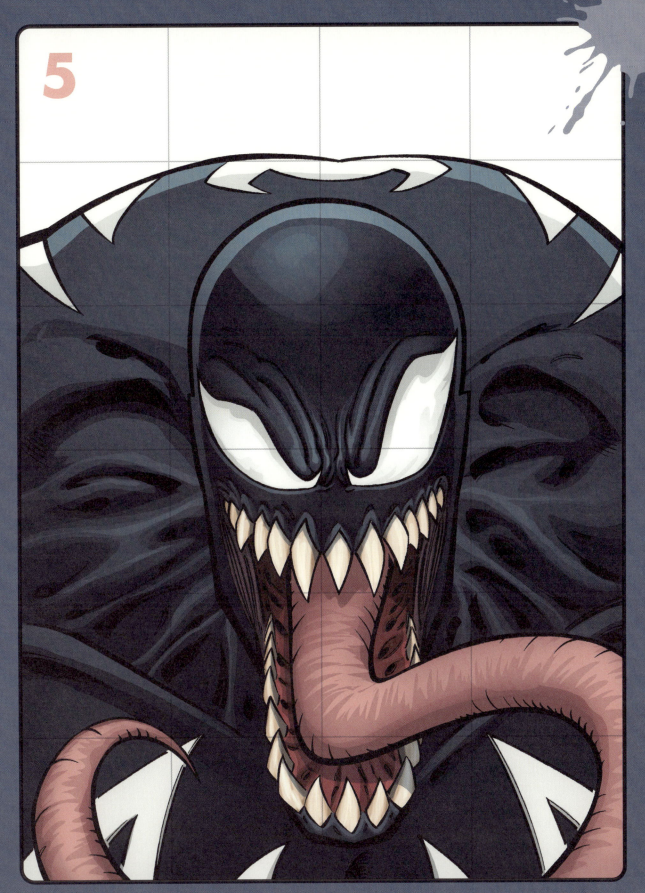

Step-by-step Method

Follow along, first drawing basic shapes with light pencil lines.

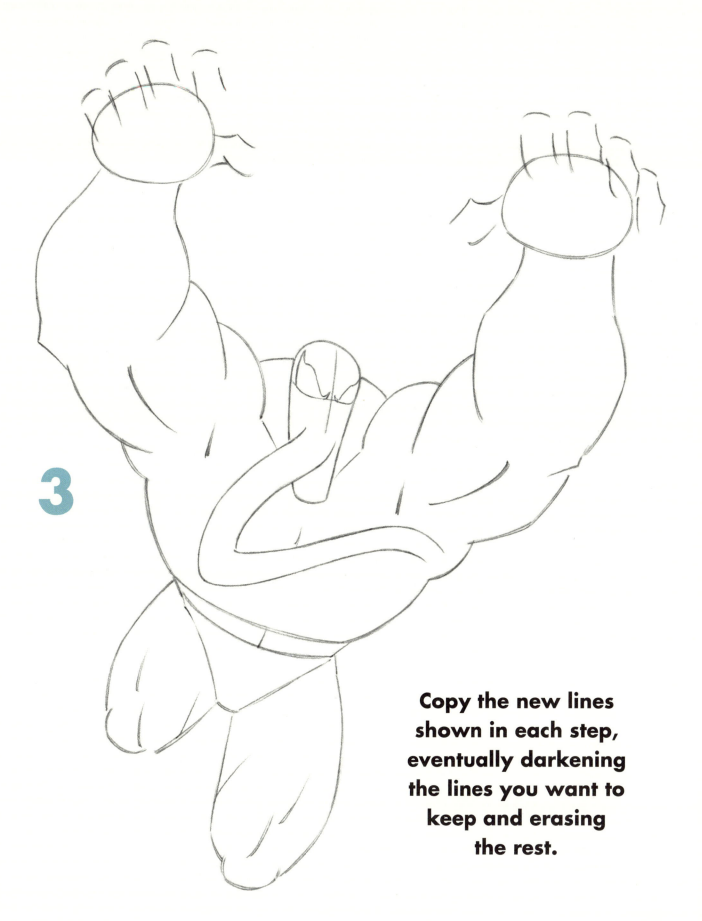

Copy the new lines shown in each step, eventually darkening the lines you want to keep and erasing the rest.

6

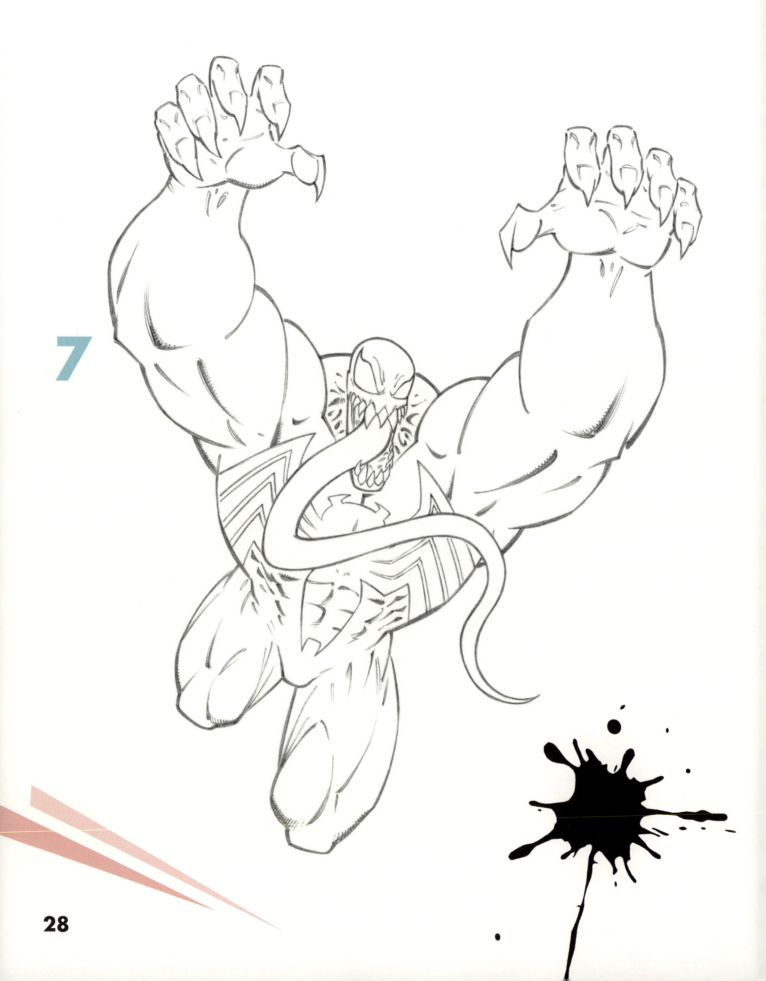

7

28

8

Add color to your drawing with colored pencils, markers, paints, or crayons.

LIZARD

Dr. Curtis Connors, a world-renowned lizard expert and gifted surgeon, becomes obsessed with uncovering the secrets of reptilian regeneration so he can grow back his arm after it is amputated. He develops a serum that includes reptile DNA, and tests it on himself. His arm does indeed grow back, but the serum has one side effect: Connors is transformed into a reptilian monster!

SUPER-POWERS

* Exceptional strength, speed, agility, and reflexes
* Tough, scaly skin offers protection
* Can regenerate damaged areas of his body
* Ability to telepathically control nearby reptiles
* Excretes pheromones that cause humans to behave violently

Tracing Method

Trace Lizard using transparent paper.

31

Grid Method

Copy the lines shown in each step. When you're done with all the steps, you'll have a complete drawing of Lizard. Color in your drawing with markers, colored pencils, crayons, or paints.

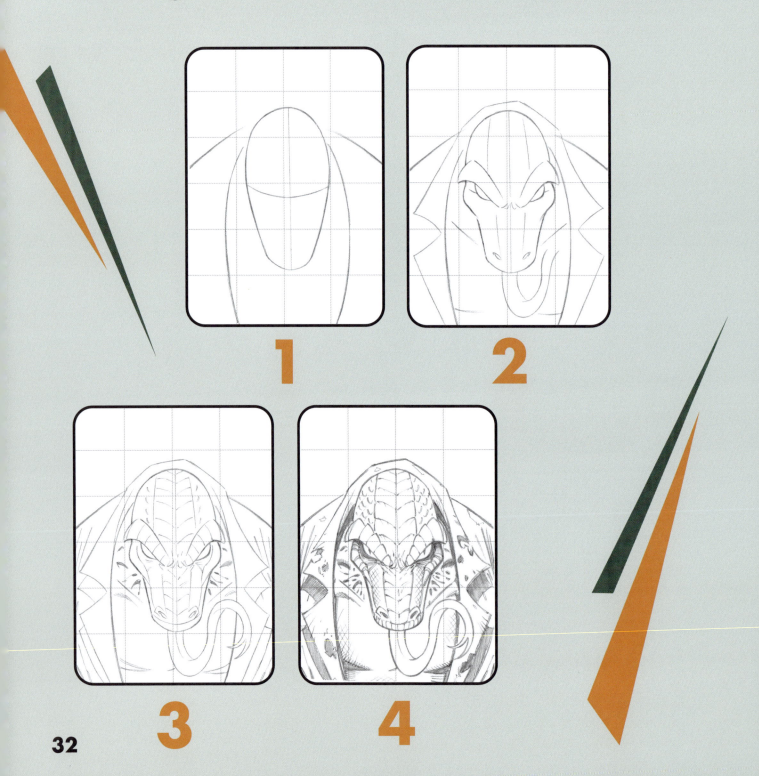

5

Step-by-step Method

Follow along, first drawing basic shapes with light pencil lines.

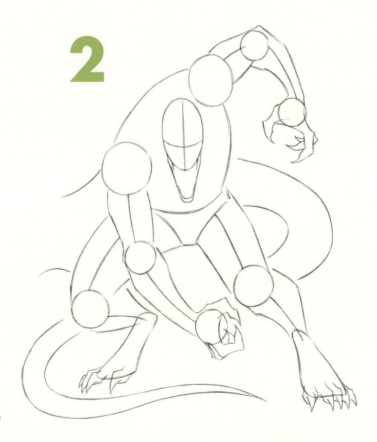

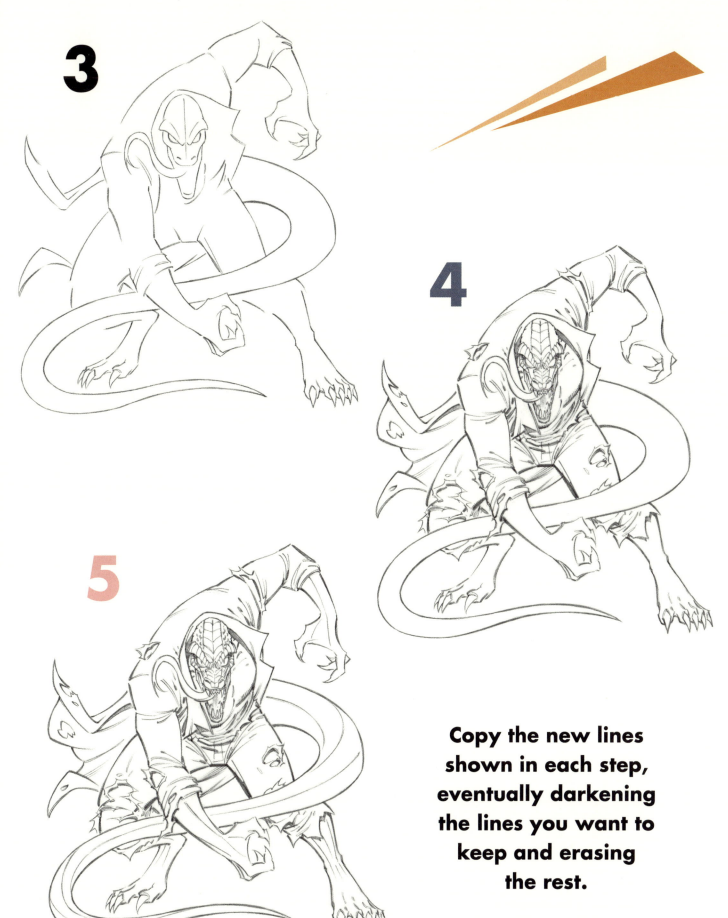

Copy the new lines shown in each step, eventually darkening the lines you want to keep and erasing the rest.

6

7

36

Add color to your drawing with colored pencils, markers, paints, or crayons.

8

37

GREEN GOBLIN

Norman Osborn is the father of Peter Parker's best friend, Harry. He is also co-owner of a chemical manufacturing, research and development company. Osborn becomes the **GREEN GOBLIN** after testing a strength-enhancing serum on himself. He emerges smarter and stronger, but uses his intelligence for evil, and causes Spider-Man more problems than any other foe.

SUPER-POWERS

✱ Intelligent and cunning businessman

✱ Enhanced strength, speed, reflexes, endurance, and healing

✱ Fights using his Goblin Glider, bombs, flying "razor bats," laser-emitting gloves, and gas that nullifies Spider-Man's spider-sense

✱ Can slowly regenerate damaged tissue and organs

Step-by-step Method

Follow along, first drawing basic shapes with light pencil lines.

Copy the new lines shown in each step, eventually darkening the lines you want to keep and erasing the rest.

39

5

Copy the new lines shown in each step, eventually darkening the lines you want to keep and erasing the rest.

6

41

7

Add color to your drawing with colored pencils, markers, paints, or crayons.

8

RHINO

Aleksei Sytsevich, a thug in the Russian mafia, is selected by professional spies for his muscular physique. They promise Aleksei wealth and power to undergo a life-threatening series of chemical and radiation treatments, which transform him into super-strong agent, **RHINO**. Aleksei's powerful armor, modeled after the hide of a rhinoceros, is permanently bonded to his body.

SUPER-POWERS

* Bulletproof, acid-resistant Rhino suit offers protection from explosions and extreme temperatures
* Indestructible horns
* Exceptional strength and speed
* High endurance and a high degree of imperviousness to physical harm

Step-by-step Method

Follow along, first drawing basic shapes with light pencil lines.

1

2

Copy the new lines shown in each step, eventually darkening the lines you want to keep and erasing the rest.

4

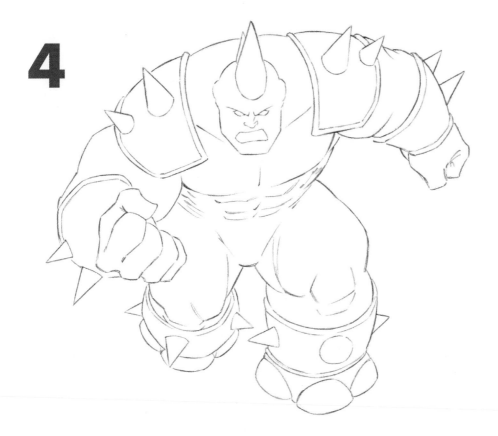

5

47

6

7

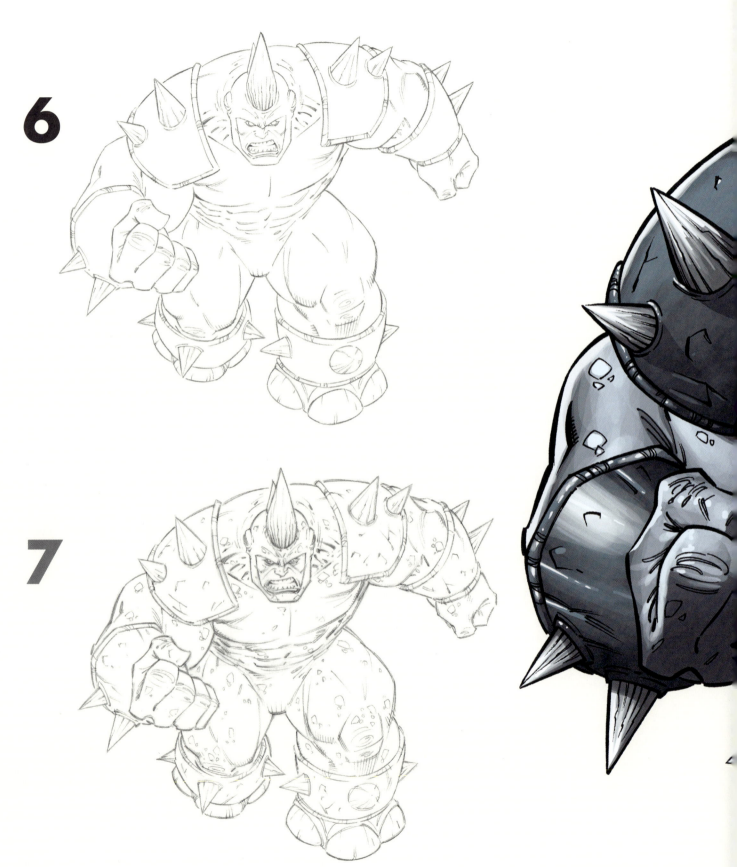

48

8

Add color to your drawing with colored pencils, markers, paints, or crayons.

DOCTOR OCTOPUS

Dr. Otto Octavius holds a PhD in nuclear science and is the world's leading authority on nuclear radiation and its effects on human physiology. He is also a brilliant engineer and inventor. However, after accidental exposure to atomic radiation, **DOCTOR OCTOPUS** now telepathically controls four dangerous mechanical arms that are fused to his body.

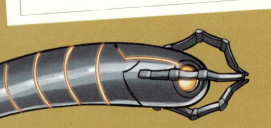

SUPER-POWERS

* Superior intellect in the field of nuclear science
* Travels quickly, scales walls, and can stand up to 50 feet in the air using his tentacles as legs
* Fights with fast, strong, and sharp tentacles
* Can "feel" basic sensations with tentacles' pincers by sensing electrical resistance

Tracing Method

Trace Doctor Octopus using transparent paper.

Step-by-step Method

Follow along, first drawing basic shapes with light pencil lines.

Copy the new lines shown in each step, eventually darkening the lines you want to keep and erasing the rest.

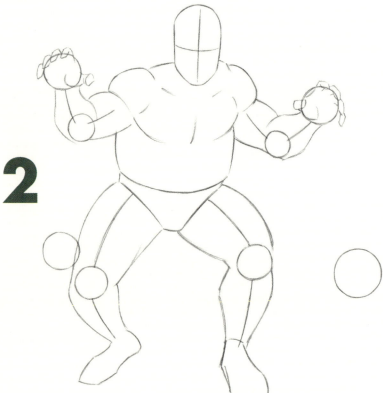

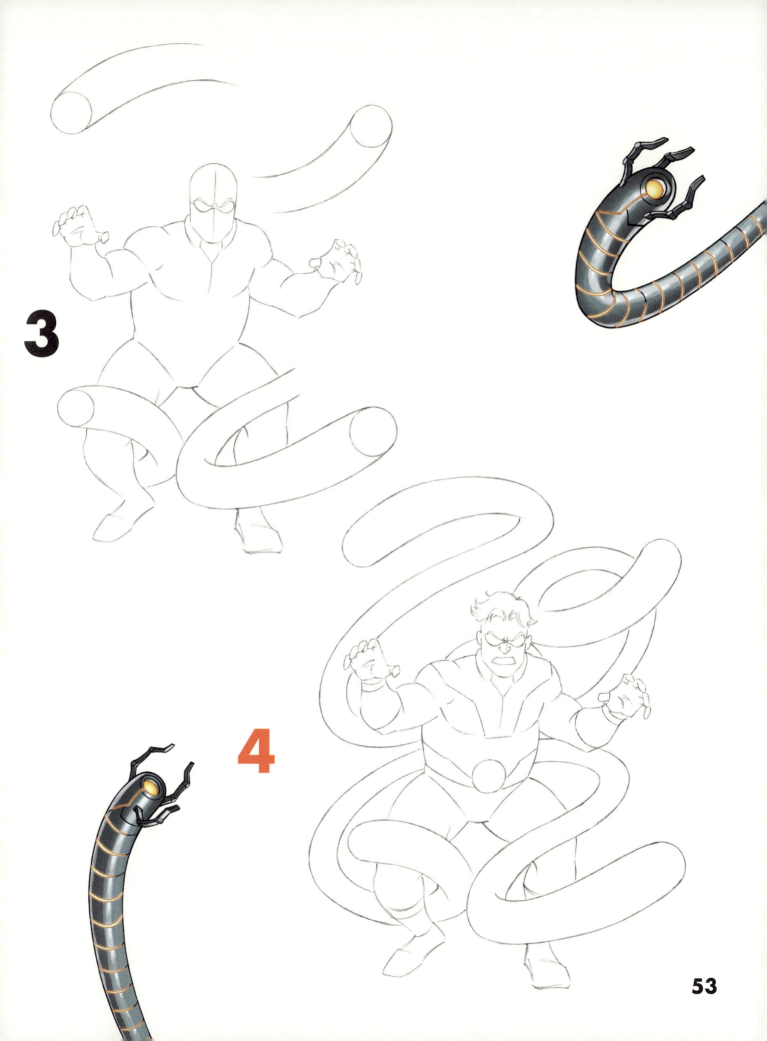

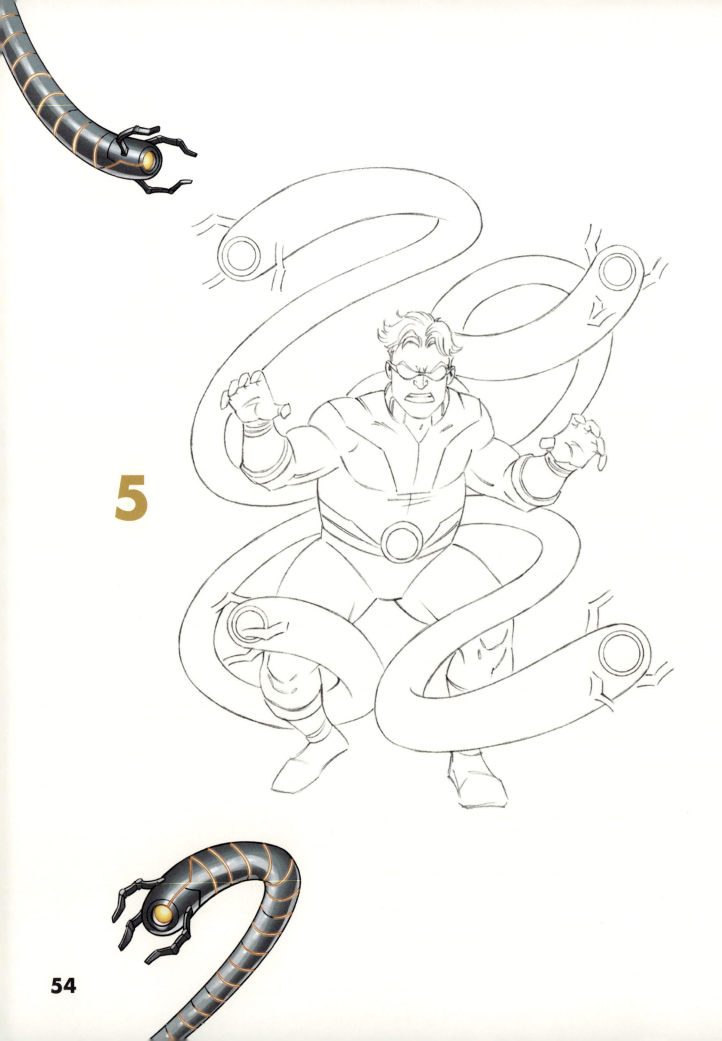

6

Add color to your drawing with colored pencils, markers, paints, or crayons.

7

IRON MAN

Billionaire businessman Tony Stark was wounded, captured, and told to build a weapon by his enemies. But instead, Tony created an advanced suit of armor to heal his wounds and escape captivity. Now, with a new outlook on life, Tony uses his money and intelligence to make the world a safer, better place as **IRON MAN**.

SUPER-POWERS

* Invents advanced weapons, including new models of his Iron Man suit

* Flies using the suit

* Uses repulsor rays, pulse bolts, mini-missiles, magnetic field generators, and more while fighting his enemies

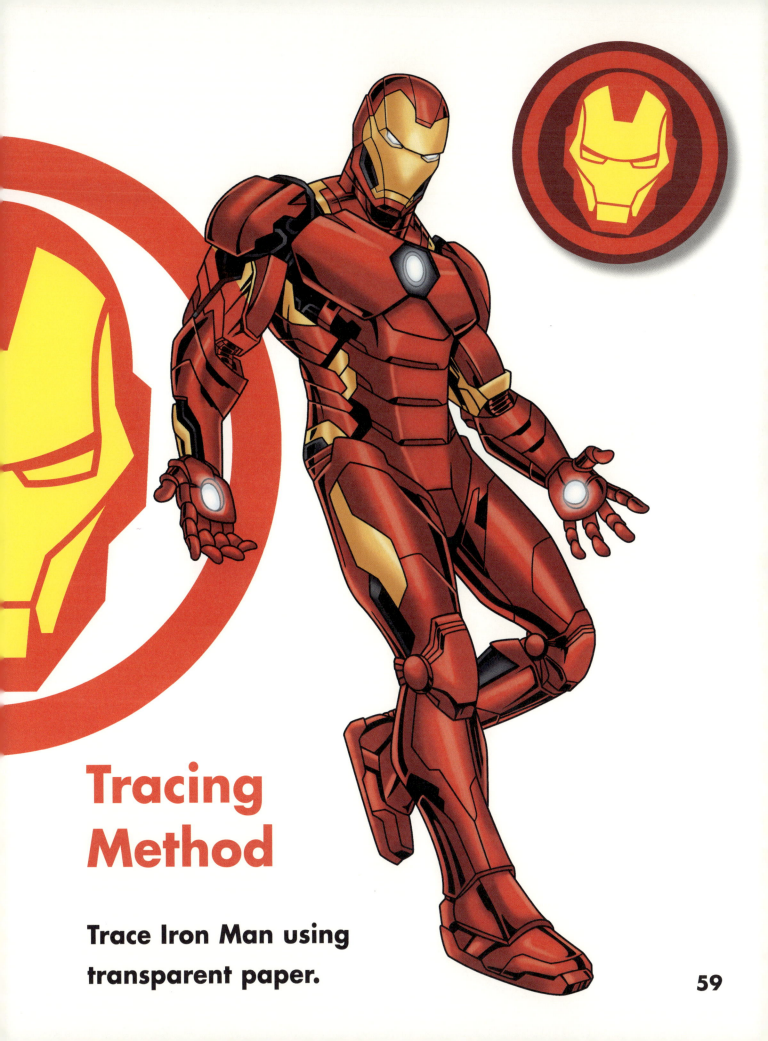

Tracing Method

Trace Iron Man using transparent paper.

59

Grid Method

Copy the lines shown in each step. When you're done with all the steps, you'll have a complete drawing of Iron Man. Color in your drawing with markers, colored pencils, crayons, or paints.

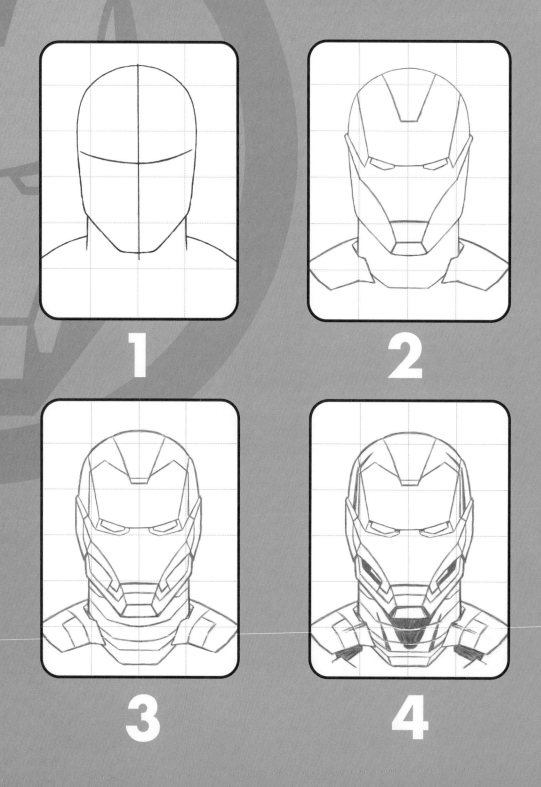

Step-by-step Method

Follow along, first drawing basic shapes with light pencil lines. Copy the new lines shown in each step, eventually darkening the lines you want to keep and erasing the rest.

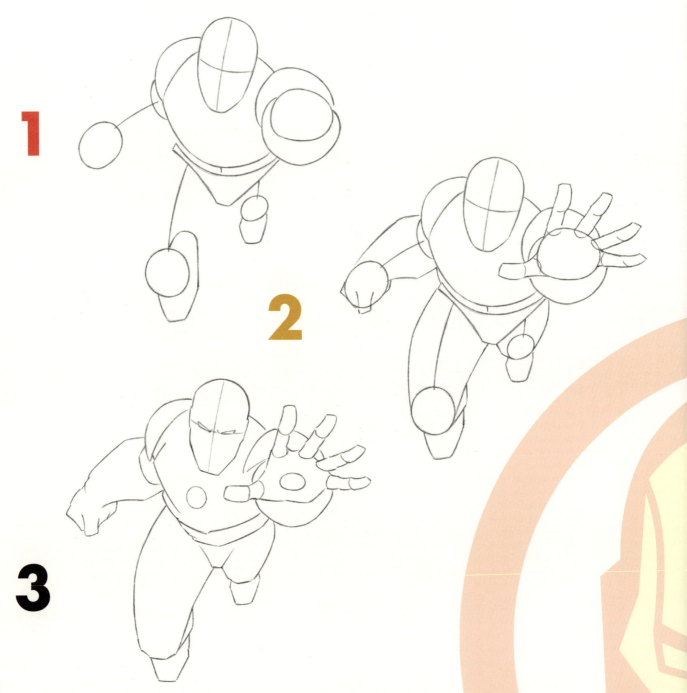

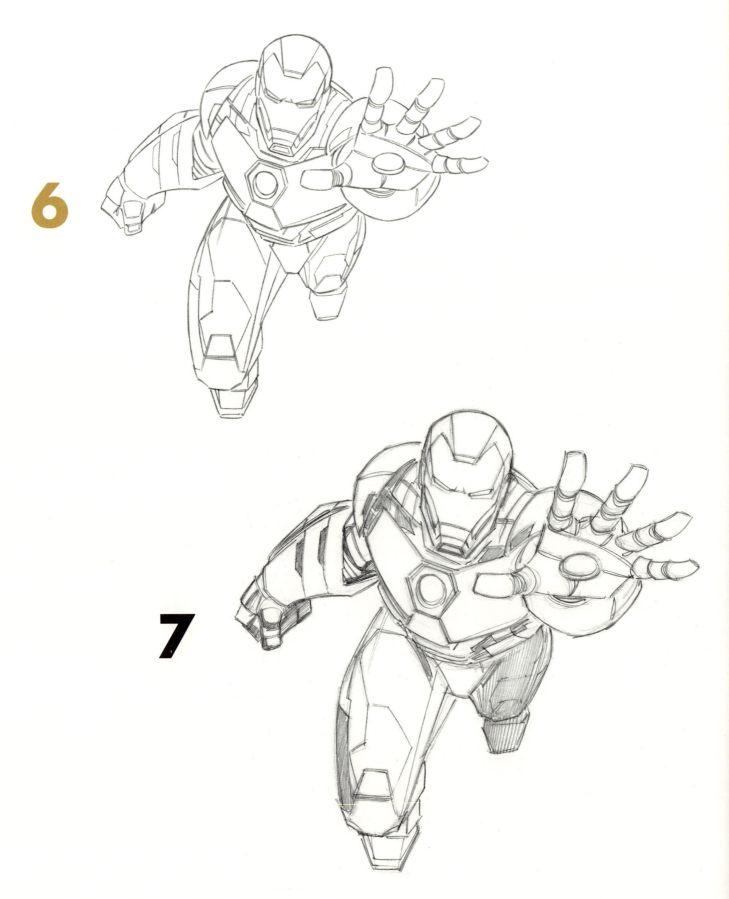

8

Add color to your drawing with colored pencils, markers, paints, or crayons.

CAPTAIN AMERICA

Vowing to serve his country any way he could, young Steve Rogers took the Super-Soldier Serum to become America's one-man army. Fighting for the red, white, and blue for more than 60 years, **CAPTAIN AMERICA** is the living, breathing symbol of freedom and liberty.

SUPER-POWERS

* Is more agile, stronger, and faster than regular soldiers
* Carries an indestructible shield that can also be used as a weapon
* Fights using his own style of hand-to-hand combat

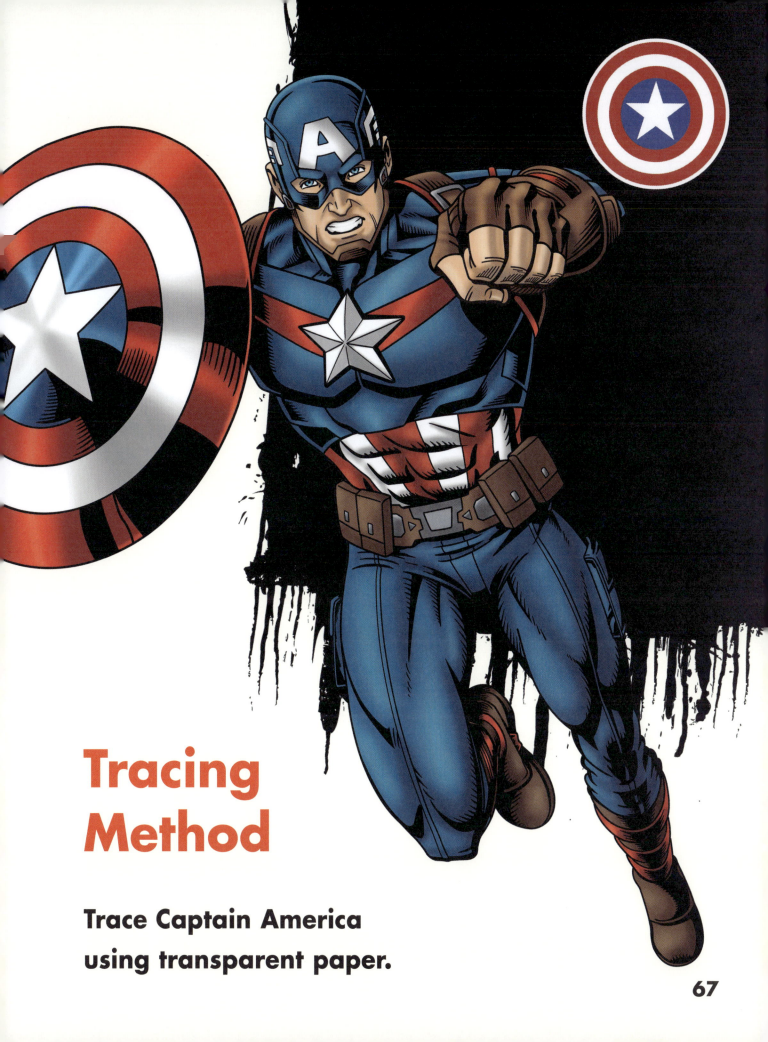

Tracing Method

Trace Captain America using transparent paper.

Grid Method

Copy the lines shown in each step. When you're done with all the steps, you'll have a complete drawing of Captain America. Color in your drawing with markers, colored pencils, crayons, or paints.

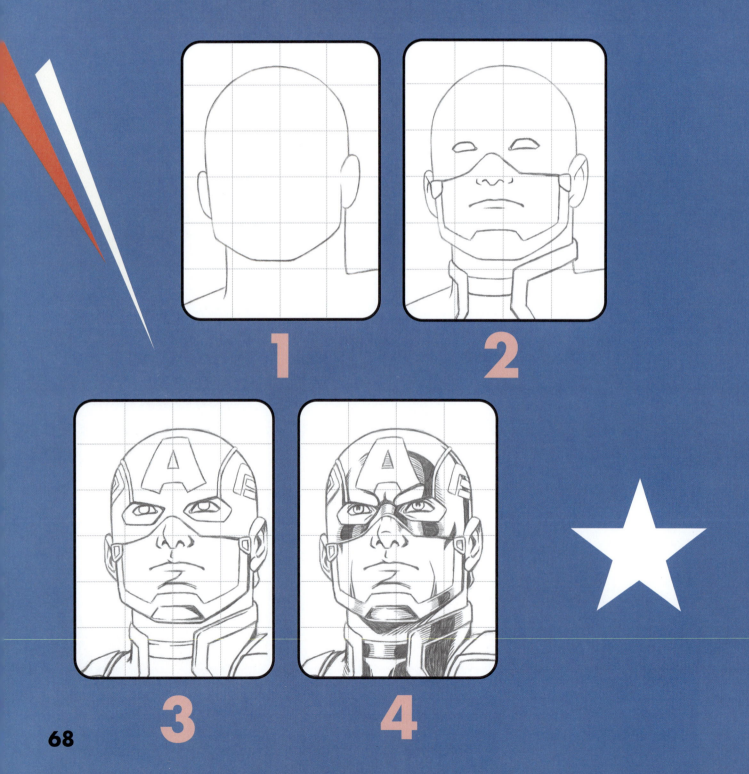

1

2

3

4

Step-by-step Method

Follow along, first drawing basic shapes with light pencil lines. Copy the new lines shown in each step, eventually darkening the lines you want to keep and erasing the rest. Finally, add color to your drawing with colored pencils, markers, paints, or crayons.

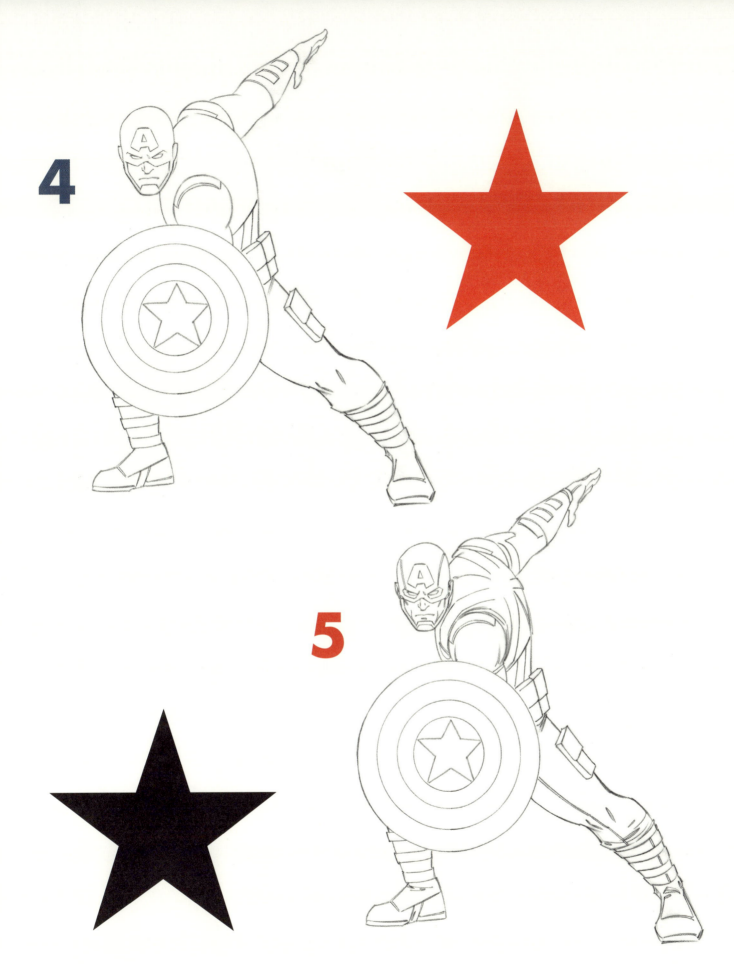

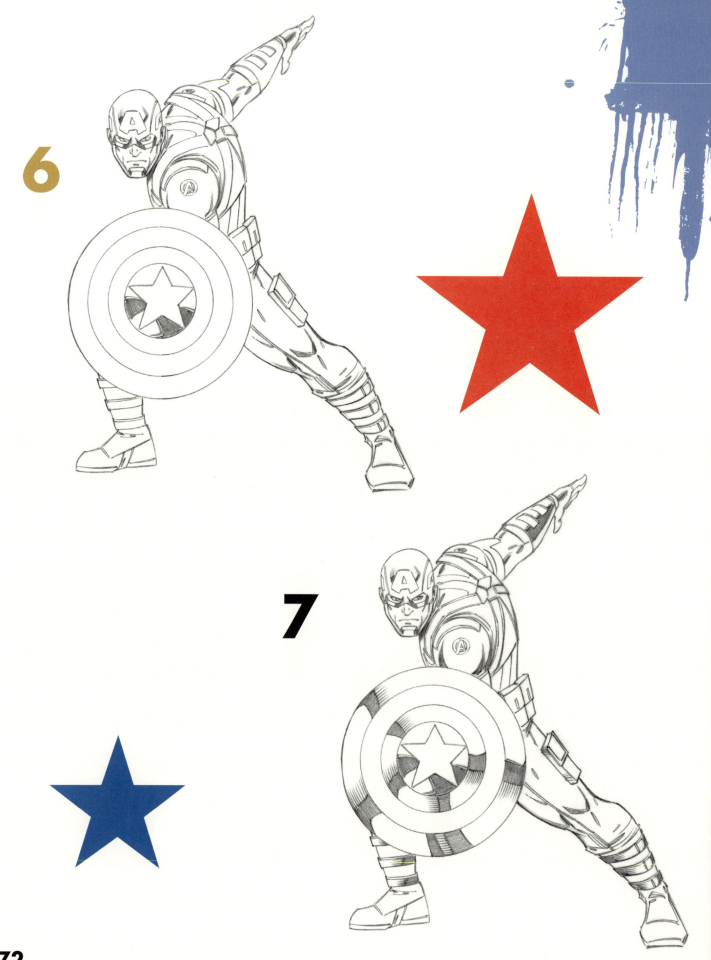

BLACK WIDOW

Natasha Romanoff is an expert spy, athlete, and assassin who goes by many aliases, including **BLACK WIDOW**. She started her training at an early age at the KGB's infamous Red Room Academy. Black Widow was formerly an enemy to the Avengers, but she later became their ally and a top S.H.I.E.L.D. agent.

SUPER-POWERS

* Is an excellent fighter and spy due to her training

* Discharges the "widow's bite," high-frequency electrostatic bolts, from her bracelets

* Carries plastic explosive discs, knives, and other weapons in her protective suit

Tracing Method

Trace Black Widow using transparent paper.

Grid Method

Copy the lines shown in each step. When you're done with all the steps, you'll have a complete drawing of Black Widow. Color in your drawing with markers, colored pencils, crayons, or paints.

5

Step-by-step Method

Follow along, first drawing basic shapes with light pencil lines. Copy the new lines shown in each step, eventually darkening the lines you want to keep and erasing the rest. Finally, add color to your drawing with colored pencils, markers, paints, or crayons.

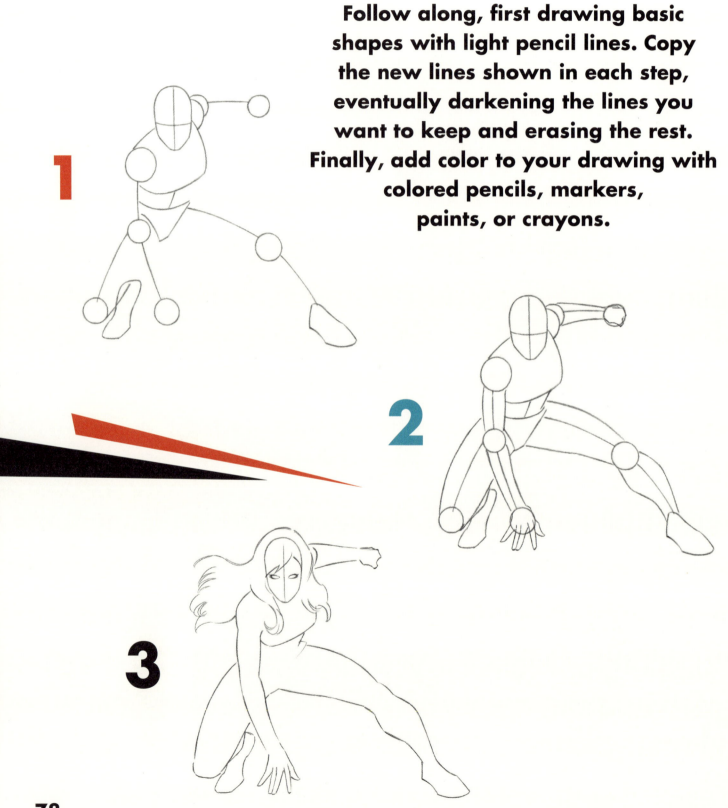

4

5

79

6

HULK

After being exposed to harmful gamma rays, Dr. Bruce Banner was transformed into the incredibly powerful creature called the **HULK**. Dr. Bruce Banner is a genius in nuclear physics, but when he is the Hulk, Banner's consciousness is buried within the Hulk's.

SUPER-POWERS

✱ Becomes stronger and stronger as his stress level increases

✱ Can leap great distances

✱ Creates shock waves by slamming his hands together—this shock wave can deafen people, send objects flying, and extinguish fires

Tracing Method

Trace Hulk using transparent paper.

Grid Method

Copy the lines shown in each step. When you're done with all the steps, you'll have a complete drawing of Hulk. Color in your drawing with markers, colored pencils, crayons, or paints.

Step-by-step Method

Follow along, first drawing basic shapes with light pencil lines. Copy the new lines shown in each step, eventually darkening the lines you want to keep and erasing the rest. Finally, add color to your drawing with colored pencils, markers, paints, or crayons.

THOR

THOR, the son of Odin and Gaea, is the Norse god of thunder and lightning. He wields one of the greatest weapons ever made, the enchanted hammer, Mjolnir. Thor is smart, compassionate, self-assured, and would never stop fighting for a worthwhile cause.

SUPER-POWERS

* Wields the powerful hammer Mjolnir forged from Uru metal—the hammer cannot be used by anyone unworthy

* Can fly using Mjolnir

* Possesses the Belt of Strength and a pair of iron gauntlets to protect him while using Mjolnir

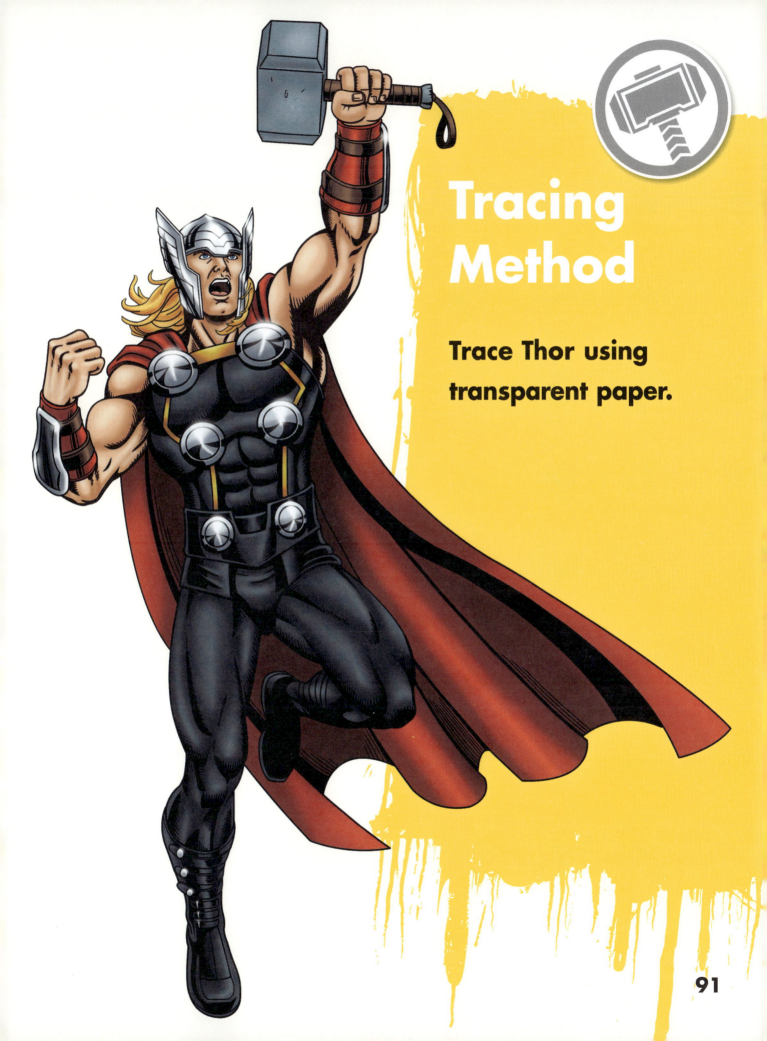

Tracing Method

Trace Thor using transparent paper.

Step-by-step Method

Follow along, first drawing basic shapes with light pencil lines. Copy the new lines shown in each step, eventually darkening the lines you want to keep and erasing the rest. Finally, add color to your drawing with colored pencils, markers, paints, or crayons.

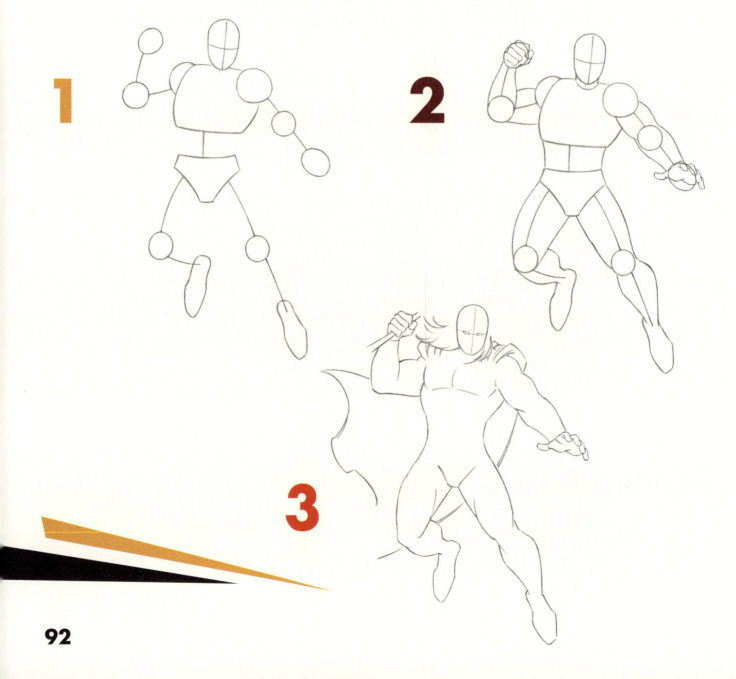

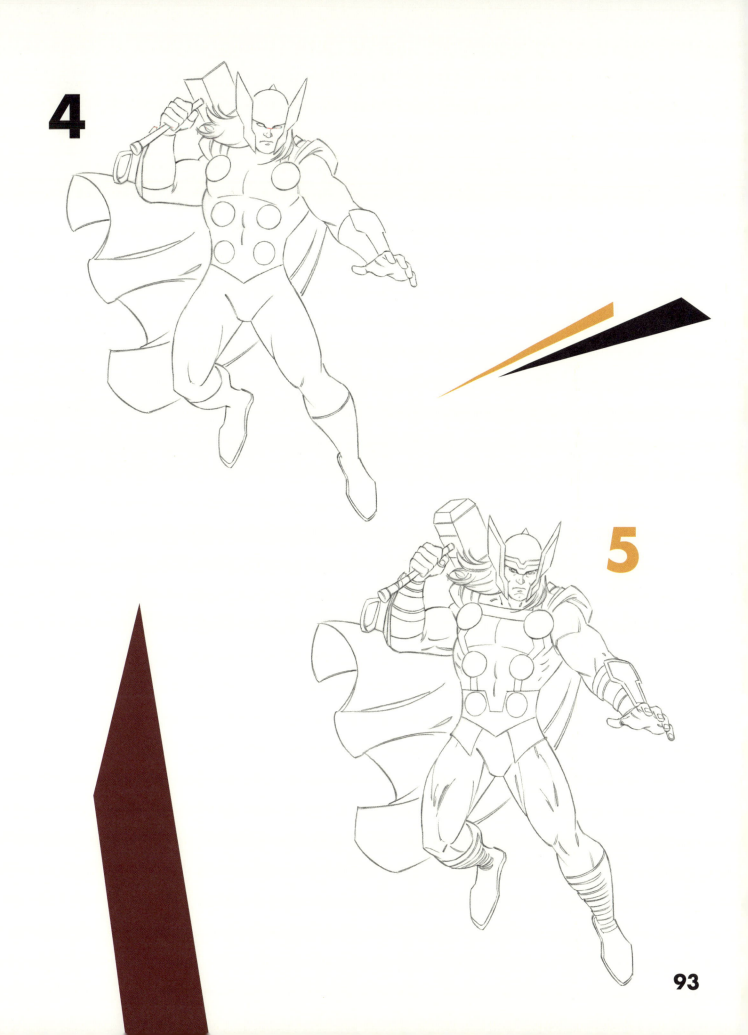

8

ANT-MAN

Scott Lang was an electronics engineer, but he turned to a life of crime. He stole Dr. Henry Pym's **ANT-MAN** suit, but Pym allowed him to keep it and Scott Lang become Ant-Man. With the suit, Scott can shrink to the size of an ant but keep the strength he has at full size.

SUPER-POWERS

* Can shrink to the size of an ant
* Has expertise in electronics
* Wears a special helmet to communicate to insects and amplify his voice so that a full-sized person can hear him

Step-by-step Method

Follow along, first drawing basic shapes with light pencil lines. Copy the new lines shown in each step, eventually darkening the lines you want to keep and erasing the rest. Finally, add color to your drawing with colored pencils, markers, paints, or crayons.

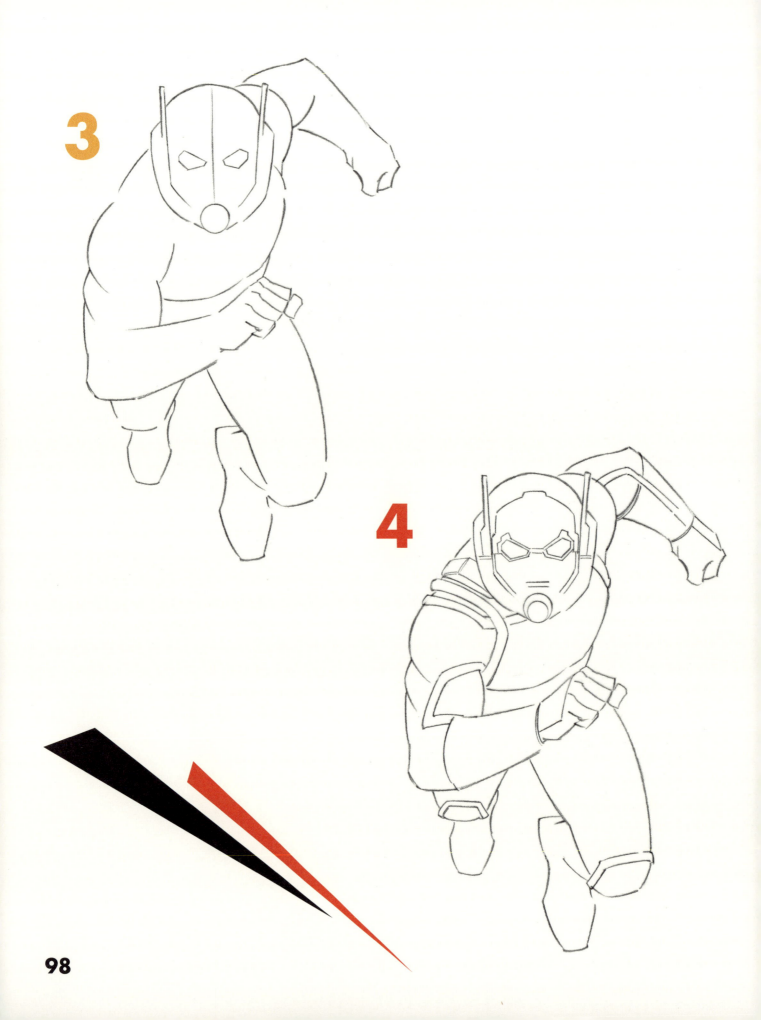

8

BLACK PANTHER

T'Challa was born the prince of Wakanda, a technologically advanced but secretive country in Africa. He underwent ritual trials and won the heart-shaped herb, which enhanced his abilities and linked him spiritually to the panther goddess, Bast. He became Wakanda's ruler as the **BLACK PANTHER** after the death of his father.

Avengers

SUPER-POWERS

* Has enhanced senses and physical ability from the heart-shaped herb
* Wears a bulletproof Vibranium-weave uniform that gives him catlike abilities
* Has access to high-tech weapons and vehicles

Step-by-step Method

Follow along, first drawing basic shapes with light pencil lines. Copy the new lines shown in each step, eventually darkening the lines you want to keep and erasing the rest. Finally, add color to your drawing with colored pencils, markers, paints, or crayons.

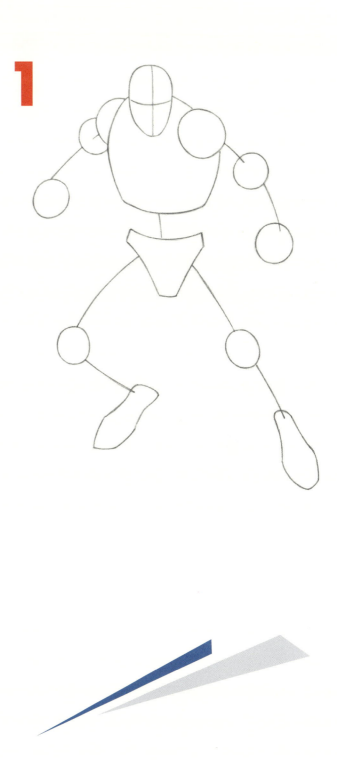

1

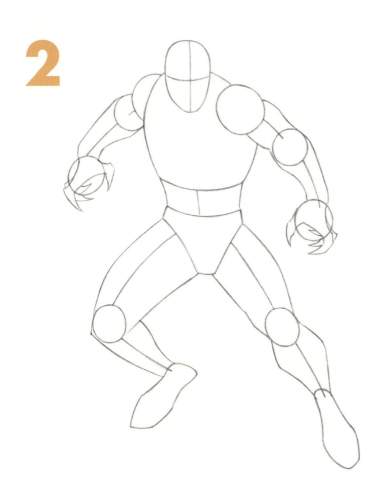

2

103

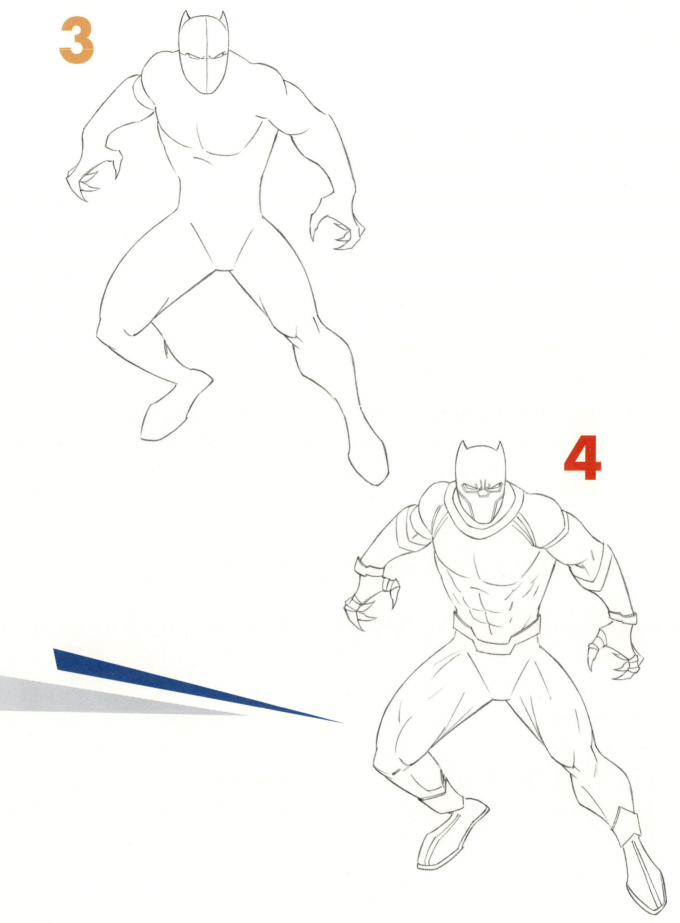

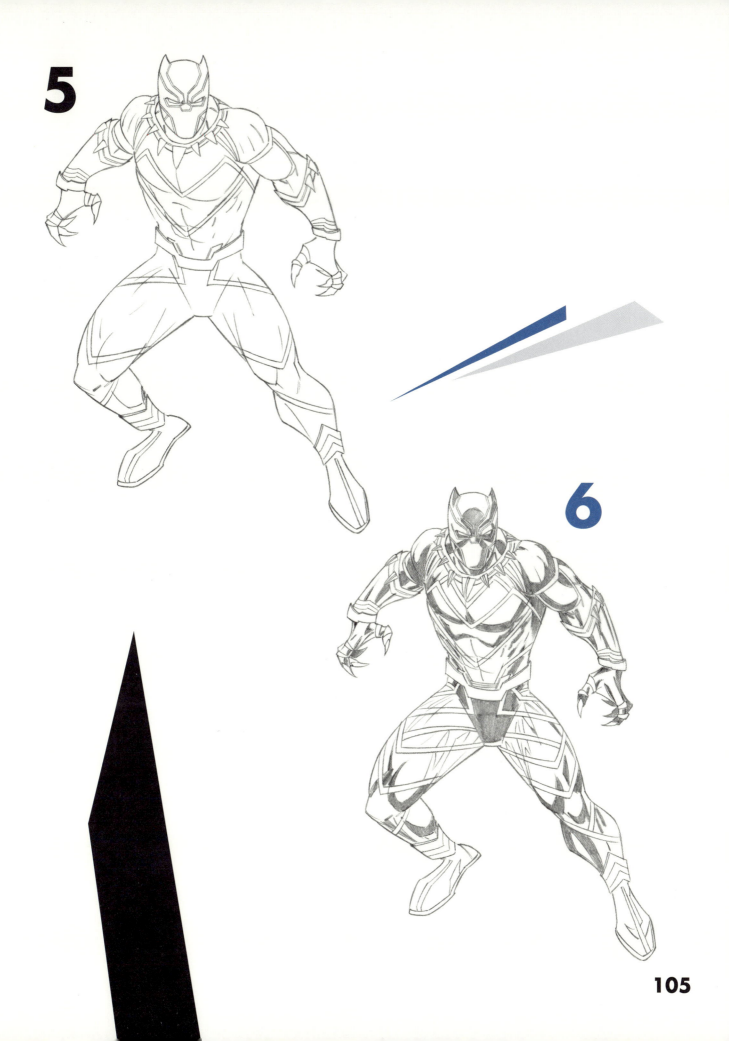

105

7

8

CAPTAIN MARVEL

Major Carol Danvers joined the C.I.A. after much success in the Air Force. On one mission, Carol was caught in the explosion of a Kree Psyche-Magnetron device with a Kree alien named Marvell. The explosion didn't kill Carol, but it caused her to become a Kree–human hybrid. With newly acquired super-powers, Carol joined the Avengers and became **CAPTAIN MARVEL**.

SUPER-POWERS

* Can fly with or without a plane
* Has enhanced strength and durability
* Shoots concussive energy bursts from her hands

Step-by-step Method

Follow along, first drawing basic shapes with light pencil lines. Copy the new lines shown in each step, eventually darkening the lines you want to keep and erasing the rest. Finally, add color to your drawing with colored pencils, markers, paints, or crayons.

1

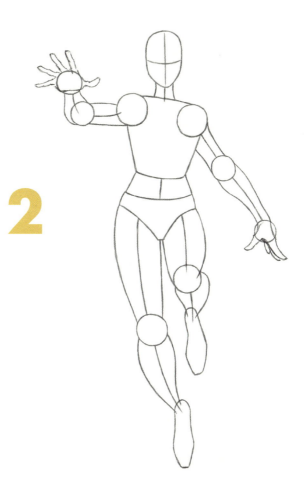

2

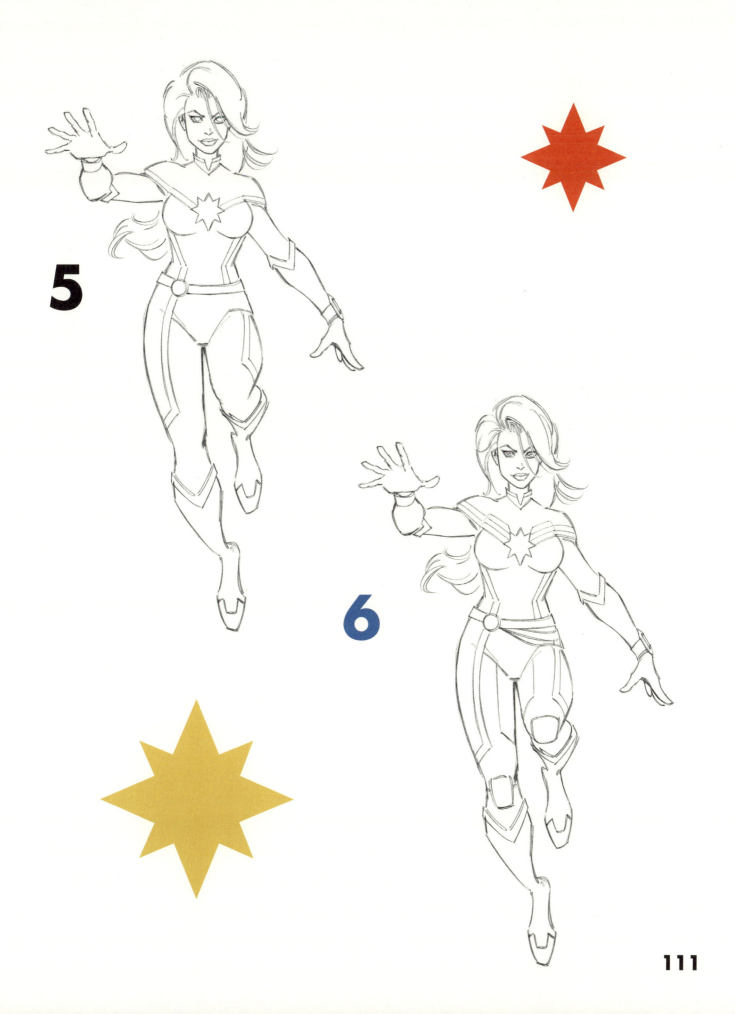

7

8

STAR-LORD

Peter Quill was taken from his home on Earth by the pirate-like Ravagers. Now a headstrong intergalactic adventurer, he travels the cosmos as **STAR-LORD** in his space ship, the Milano. Equipped with a high-tech blaster and a mix-tape of music from home, Star-Lord leads an unlikely team of interstellar misfits—the Guardians of the Galaxy—as they seek their fortune.

SUPER-POWERS

* Unique blaster that works only in his hands
* High-tech mask with a variety of vision modes
* Enhanced healing
* Personal energy shields
* Can see all energy spectra with cybernetic implant
* 100% memory recall
* Gifted strategist, thinks outside the box
* Skilled marksman and swordsman

Tracing Method

Trace Star-Lord using transparent paper.

115

Grid Method

Copy the lines shown in each step. When you're done with all the steps, you'll have a complete drawing of Star-Lord. Color in your drawing with markers, colored pencils, crayons, or paints.

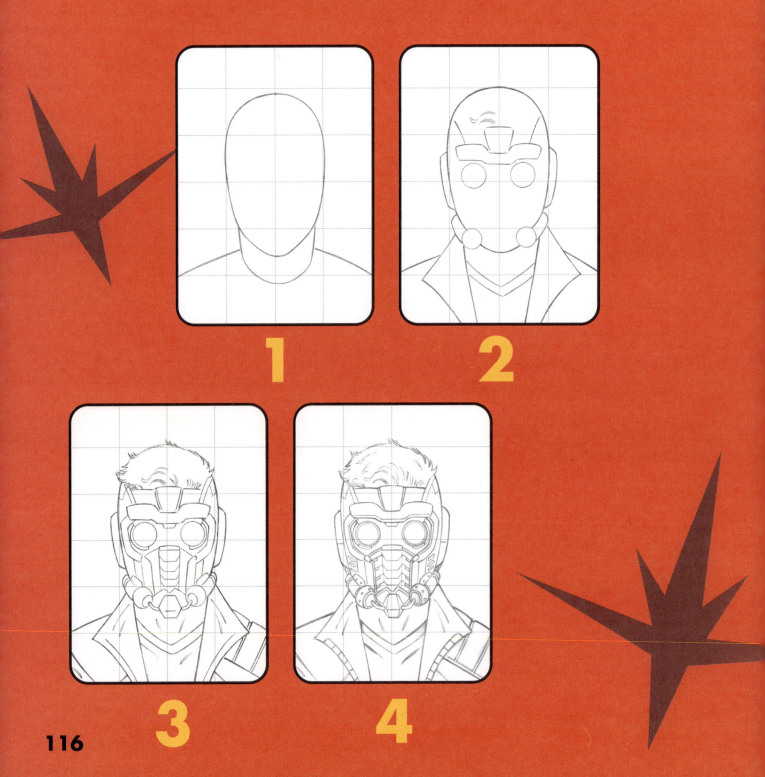

Step-by-step Method

Follow along, first drawing basic shapes with light pencil lines. Copy the new lines shown in each step, eventually darkening the lines you want to keep and erasing the rest.

1

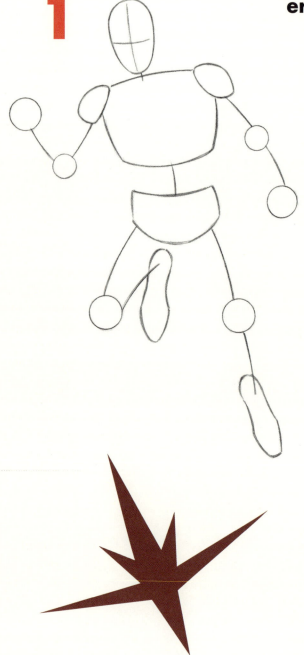

2

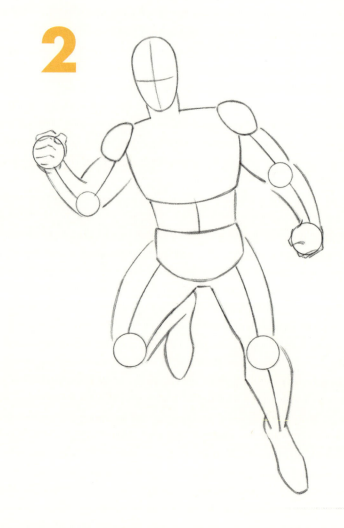

8

Add color to your drawing with colored pencils, markers, paints, or crayons.

123

GAMORA

GAMORA was raised by the tyrant Thanos, after the rest of her species was annihilated. She was trained as an unparalleled warrior, but weary of the crimes she was forced to commit by Thanos, Gamora broke free. Now, she puts her extraordinary skills to use as a member of the Guardians of the Galaxy, seeking to redeem the wrongdoings of her past.

SUPER-POWERS

* Master of hand-to-hand combat
* Proficient in a wide variety of weaponry, including blasters and swords
* Highly skilled in the art of subterfuge
* Increased strength, agility, physical conditioning, and healing
* Cybernetic implants
* Genetic alteration

Tracing Method

Trace Gamora using transparent paper.

125

Step-by-step Method

Follow along, first drawing basic shapes with light pencil lines. Copy the new lines shown in each step, eventually darkening the lines you want to keep and erasing the rest.

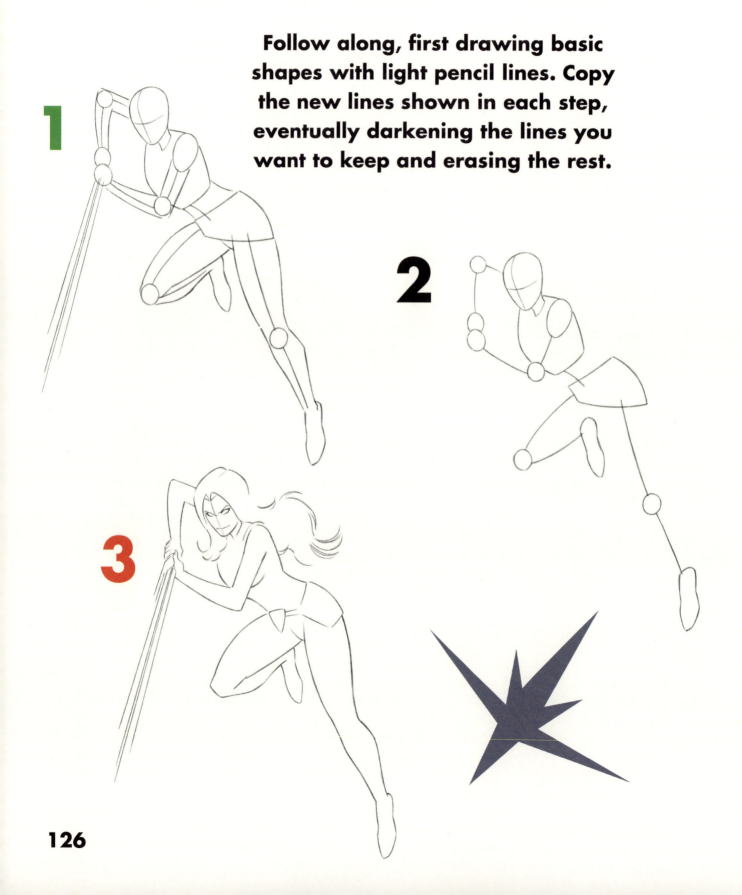

8

Add color to your drawing with colored pencils, markers, paints, or crayons.

ROCKET

He looks like a common Earth raccoon, but **ROCKET** is in fact a one-of-a-kind being, created on the planet Halfworld. This diminutive, tough-talking creature is a master pilot, engineer, marksman, and weapons specialist. Previously a small-time thief along with his partner, Groot, Rocket was unable to resist the call of adventure. He now lends his genius and heavy artillery to the Guardians of the Galaxy.

SUPER-POWERS

* Genetically and cybernetically enhanced
* Highly agile
* Mechanical genius, with particular aptitude in engineering, vehicles, and heavy munitions
* Intuitive ability to pilot most vehicles

Tracing Method

Trace Rocket using transparent paper.

Step-by-step Method

Follow along, first drawing basic shapes with light pencil lines. Copy the new lines shown in each step, eventually darkening the lines you want to keep and erasing the rest.

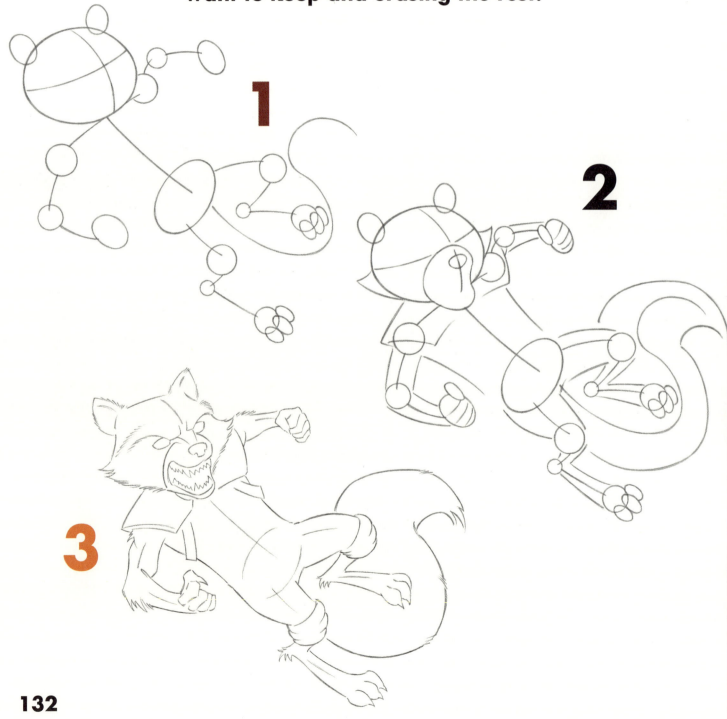

8

Add color to your drawing with colored pencils, markers, paints, or crayons.

GROOT

GROOT is a member of a super-strong, tree-like alien race. Usually he is calm and quiet, but he can unleash his tremendous strength on any enemy who threatens his allies, particularly his long-time partner in crime, Rocket, and the other Guardians of the Galaxy. He can only say, "I am Groot," but the gentle giant's friends can always understand exactly what he means.

SUPER-POWERS

* **Superhuman strength**
* **Ability to regenerate after physical damage**
* **Plant-like form enables him to grow or reshape his limbs and root himself in place for enhanced stability**
* **Can emit glowing spores**

Tracing Method

Trace Groot using transparent paper.

Step-by-step Method

1

Follow along, first drawing basic shapes with light pencil lines. Copy the new lines shown in each step, eventually darkening the lines you want to keep and erasing the rest.

2

3

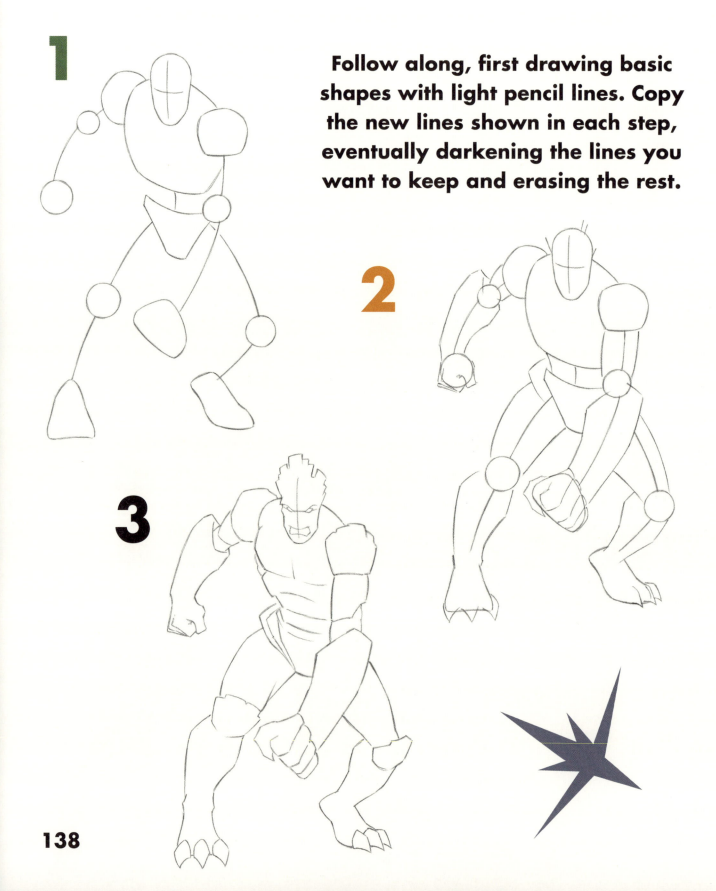

138

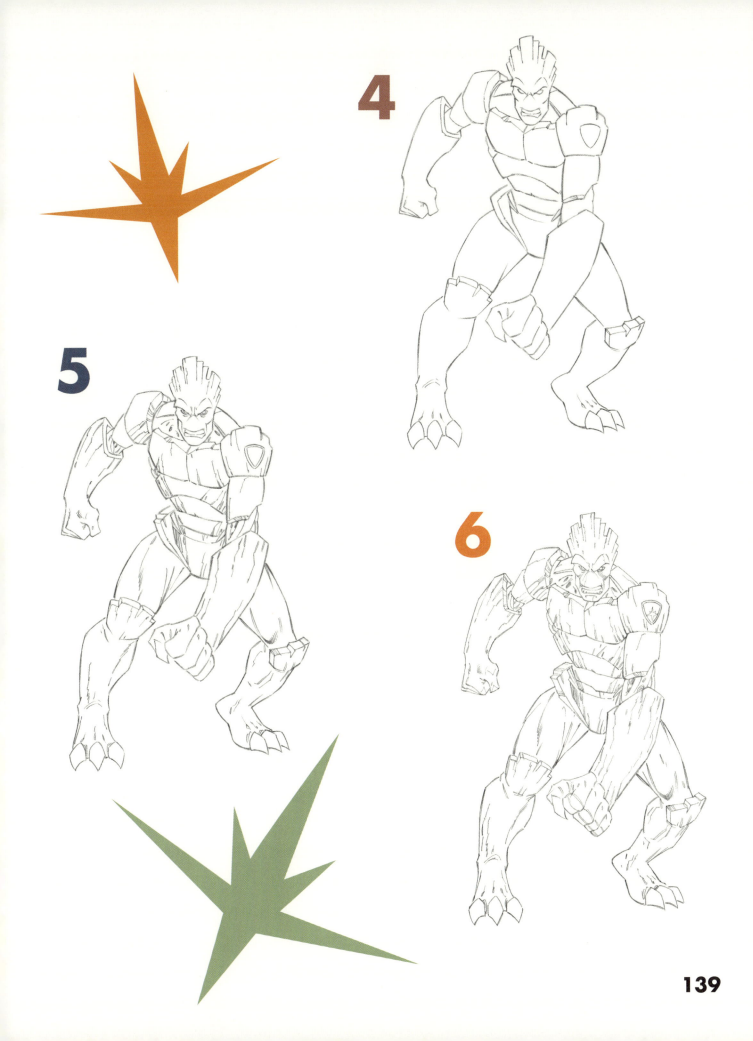

8

Add color to your drawing with colored pencils, markers, paints, or crayons.

YOUNG GROOT

Grid Method

Copy the lines shown in each step. When you're done with all the steps, you'll have a complete drawing of Young Groot. Color in your drawing with markers, colored pencils, crayons, or paints.

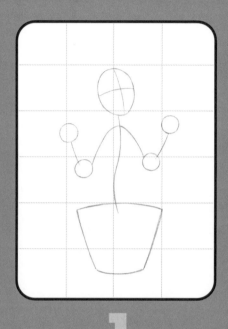
1

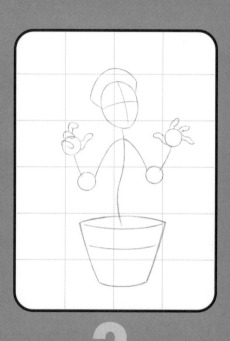
2

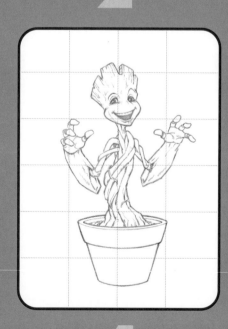
3

4

Don't miss other How to Draw books